$^1/_2$ Minute Meditations

Anyone *can do* *Anywhere*

A simple practice to calm emotions and sharpen focus
or expand intuition and enhance creativity

Mischa V Alyea

The Publisher: Aashni Spiritual Living

Kansas City, MO 64118

USA

Website: www.AashniSpiritualLiving.com

Email: AashniSpiritualLiving@gmail.com

ISBN: 0692412638

ISBN-13: 978-0692412633

Publisher's Note

This publication is designed to provide accurate and authoritative information in regard to the subject matter covered. It is sold with the understanding that the publisher is not engaged in rendering psychological or medical services. If expert counseling or medical assistance is needed, the services of a competent professional should be sought.

Table of Contents

Awareness 35

How to Use this Book

How to Use this Book

Some people need to relax, but cannot sit still. Some need to be energized, but can't leave their seat at work. Are you constantly on the move? Are you confined to a desk all day? Is the voice in your head your biggest stumbling block? Some need to find a way to refocus after constant interruptions so that they can get that endless to-do list done.

Science is debunking the Right-brain/Left-brain theory. Our brains do not just function on one side or the other. Brain scanning technology is showing that the brain has three networks or circuits that determine the brain's personality type:

The Brain's Three Networks

- The Executive Attention Network – Focus and Linear Thinking
- The Imagination Network – Runs Mental Simulations, Creativity, and Empathy(Emotions)
- The Internal Salience Network – Inner Awareness and Outer Movements

So, your mind's personality type really does run in circuits or circles. By running day after day on the same path, it creates a deeply grooved track that takes conscious effort to escape. When all three of these networks are running at the same time, our minds cannot function at full capacity. It's like when a computer is trying to process too much data at the same time. What meditation does is to consciously change the path that the mind is traveling. It shuts down that rut and opens a new way of thinking and experiencing life.

In order for Creative Types to improve clarity and boost productivity they need to improve concentration and focus and strengthen the executive attention network. By diverting the attention away from the dramatic re-runs and endless possibilities, a Creative Type can clear the brain of clutter. These little diversions will train the brain and get it off the emotional roller-coaster. The Concentration category is segmented into Breath, Observation, Walking, and Silent Mantra.

In order for Intellectual Types to expand their intuition and jump-start their creativity they need to open their awareness and strengthen the imagination network of the brain. When we start to see the endless possibilities in the small moments of our lives, we train the brain to look for these possibilities everywhere. The Awareness category of meditations is also segmented into Breath, Observation, Walking, and Silent Mantra.

Stress reduction and calmness are the natural results of choosing a meditation that strengthens the weaker circuit of the brain. If you are an Intellectual Type and pick a Concentration style meditation it will make your intellectual tendencies even sharper, which will dig the executive attention network rut even deeper, and take you further away from the creative brain circuit. Such practices will solidify your present judgments and make it even harder for intuition and creativity to bloom.

If you are a Creative Type and pick an Awareness style meditation, you will enhance the creative structures of the brain, which will trigger emotional turmoil and add mind clutter. Such practices will scatter the focus even further, making it that much harder to accomplish tasks and find serenity.

This book is organized so that you can quickly find a meditation practice that will work for you. If you already know your brain's personality type, then you can jump directly into the practices. If you are not sure, the first step is to take The Simple Test. It will help you to determine which category of meditation will bring the most benefit to your brain's personality type. The second segment of the test will go through your personal situation. In this way, you can further narrow down the choices of viable meditations.

There are several choices of meditation. If a practice does not work for you, choose another on the list. Meditation is meant to bring positive benefit. If you find that a meditation is not helping you, or ceases to advance your progress, feel free to move to another meditation. Jump around until you find a type that works for you.

If at sometime you wish to deepen your meditation experience by attending a class or finding a spiritual advisor, you will already know what category and type of meditation works for you and can seek out a teacher that specializes in that style.

Simple Test

Simple Test

Why are you seeking a meditation practice? You have to be very honest with yourself. These answers will guide you to a meditation that will bring beneficial change into your life.

Group A

1. Y_____ N_____ Can you see the Big Picture, but can't figure out the details to get you there?
2. Y_____ N_____ Is worry or anxiety a problem
3. Y_____ N_____ Does your mind sift through an overwhelming number of possibilities?
4. Y_____ N_____ Does your mind like to replay negative scenarios?
5. Y_____ N_____ Are you looking to be more organized?

Group B

6. Y_____ N_____ Would you like to open your creativity?

7. Y_____ N_____ Do you need more energy?

8. Y_____ N_____ Do you have a hard time seeing the Big Picture?

9. Y_____ N_____ Are your standards hard for others to live up to?

10. Y_____ N_____ Would you like to see the benefits other perspectives or possibilities could provide?

Number of times you answered *Yes* in Group A_____

Number of times you answered *Yes* in Group B_____

Those who answered *Yes* to more questions in Group A have a Creative Brain Personality. You will benefit from the Concentration category of meditations. These meditations narrow the mind's focus, keeping the attention in the present moment.

Those who answered *Yes* to more questions in Group B have an Intellectual Brain Personality. You will benefit from the Awareness category of meditations. These meditations expand the mind's focus, which creates an inclusive view of the world.

If your answers were split between the two groups, choose the category that had the most *Yes* answers.

What circumstances are in your life?

Breath meditations can be done anywhere, needs no tools, and when you are in a public place no one will know that you are meditating. Breath meditation can be done while waiting in line, sitting at a stop light in your car, or at your desk. Breath meditations are listed first because they are the most versatile of the meditation practices. Breath meditations can also be combined with other types of meditation like walking and observing.

If you would like to bring meditation into the normal activities of life, then **Observation meditation** is for you. Observation meditations consist of watching the many facets of your mind, emotions, and actions without judgment or getting caught up in the action. Observing can be done as a concentration exercise or an awareness exercise. It can incorporate a narrow focus or a panoramic view. Observation meditations are added to regular activities like washing the dishes, taking a shower, and falling asleep.

If you are constantly on the move or just can't sit still, **Walking meditations** are for you. You can incorporate walking meditations when you are moving from your car into a building, walking to the mailbox, grabbing a document off the printer, or picking up around the house.

If you would like to reprogram that nasty little voice in your head, **Silent**

Mantra meditations are for you. Silent Mantra uses "mind speak" as a way of meditation. The continuous repeating of the same words embeds the chosen phrase and way of being into our minds.

Progress is impossible

without change

and those who cannot change their minds

cannot change anything.

-George Bernard Shaw

Introduction

Chapter 0

Introduction

Too often we think that relaxation is only possible when we are on vacation. Yet our lives become chaotic and harried if our body is stressed and our mind is filled with imaginary hate mail. The good news is that we don't have to live that way. Each meditation is like a mini-vacation. It is possible to calm ourselves while we are in the midst of a chaotic moment or expand our thinking while problem-solving at work. When we reconnect to the flow of life, it makes everyday living sweeter.

Our minds have a tendency to behave like excited puppies that cannot sit still and who chew on everything that is within sight. The mind gnaws on the bones of yesterday's calamities and works itself into a tizzy of stress and negative thinking. It wishes for tomorrow, but forgets to enjoy today.

Meditation is like puppy training - but for the mind. We must teach our minds to "sit" and "stay." Another trick our mind can learn is to "retrieve." We want it to go out and find a solution that is hiding in the creative subconscious and bring it back into our conscious awareness.

Like a little puppy, our minds do not learn these skills the first time they are presented. Meditation needs to be consistent and done on a regular basis. Each meditation session ingrains the intent of the training, which continues after the meditation has ended. Consider the benefits of giving your puppy-mind five training moments as compared to one long training moment. That is why many very short sessions of meditation throughout the day can work as well as one hour-long session. When you notice the mind chasing another rabbit, do not fight it or criticize yourself. Gently call your puppy-mind back with your favorite mini-vacation.

It is important to find ways to remind yourself to meditate. The best way to start a habit and notice progress is to keep track of what you have experienced. Having a journal in your purse or on your nightstand will remind you to stop for a ½ Minute and practice. I have kept a meditation journal for many years. I am amazed at how far I have come. When I first started meditating, I tried all types of journals. I was so dissatisfied with the available journals that I created a whole line of journals that are available on Amazon.com. Each journal has spaces for all the things I like to track.

Starting a habit can be as easy as doing a meditation every time you grab your keys, every time you are waiting in line, or every time you sit down at your desk. Another way to remind yourself is to set an alarm. You can even put a sign on your desk that has the word, "Breathe!" in big letters.

You can invite a friend to be a meditation buddy. After you complete a meditation, you can send them a message telling them about your meditation. This will remind them to meditate. They will do the same for you. You can then compare notes to see what changes meditation has brought into your lives.

The best part is that any activity can be turned into an opportunity to meditate. The little snippets of the day spent riding mass transit, sitting at a stoplight, or waiting for the microwave to ding can now become useful and used for meditation practice. It is possible to deepen our everyday experiences. As we do so, we change the mundane activities of our existence into a richer and more satisfying life.

Meditating

is like lifting weights

or exercising for the mind.

Anyone can be happy

by simply

training the brain

-Mattieu Ricard

Concentration
Meditations

1

Breath Meditations

Concentration

Chapter 1

Breath Meditations

Super Calmer - Calming

What to do:

Breathe in through the nose for the count of 4. Breathe out through the mouth for the count of 4. Continue for 7-8 breaths.

Alternating Nostril Breathing - Calming

What to do:

Use the index finger of the right hand and close the right nostril. Breathe in for 4 counts. Breathe in as fully as you possibly can. Remove the right index finger. Now put the index finger of the left hand on the left nostril. Breathe out for 4 counts. Breathe out as fully as you can. Continue alternating for 7 repetitions. Switch it up! Start with the left side and see if that gives a different result.

Belly Breathing - Calming

What to do:

Place one hand on your chest and one hand on your belly. Breath in so that the belly expands, but the chest does not move. Exhale completely – sucking in your belly as small as it will go. Continue to breath deeply for 7-8 breaths.

If the belly will not expand, then try this laying face down on the floor. Breath so that the expansion of the belly lifts you off the floor slightly.

Breathing to an Even Count - Calming

What to do:

As you breathe in, count to 4. When you breathe out count to 4. Keep the breath controlled to this even rhythm for 7 breaths. As you become more acclimated, try to increase the count to 6 and then 8 to get deeper longer breaths. If you should ever feel dizzy, stop the exercise. When you return to this exercise, reduce the count.

Just Stop - Relaxing

How to do:

Stop everything you are doing. Freeze. Belly breathe. Relax your shoulders. Relax you mouth and jaw. Stay as still as you can. Then get on with your day as normal.

Breathing into Pain - Relaxing

What to do:

Gently stretch the part of the body that is painful. As you breath into the stretched area imagine that relaxation, oxygen and blood are moving to help heal this pain. As you exhale, imagine that all that is hampering this area is being washed out of the body. Do not judge the pain. It is just a messenger telling you that something needs attention.

Lion Breath - Relaxing

What to do:

Bring your shoulders up to your ears with the arms from the shoulders to the elbows clinched to your sides. Hands clinched into a fist out in front of you. Scrunch up your face with eyes squeezed shut. Exhale loudly and forcefully while you drop your shoulders, thrust your fingers out, raise your eyebrows, and stick out your tongue. The idea is to look like a lion roaring.

Counting Breaths - Focus

What to do:

Breathe as you normally breathe. Breathe in then out - count 1. Breathe in and out again – count 2. If your mind wanders and loses count, begin again at one. Stay focused and do not beat yourself up. Just begin again with no judgment. The goal is to count up to 7 or 8.

Holding between Inhale and Exhale - Focus

What to do:

Breathe in through the nose for a count of 4. Hold the breath for the count of 4. Breathe out through the nose for a count of 4. Hold the breath for a count of 4. Breathe in through the nose for a count of 4. Continue for 7-8 breaths.

Breathing to a Syncopated Count - Focus

What to do:

As you breathe in, count to 8. When you breathe out count to 4. Keep the breath controlled to this syncopated rhythm for 6-8 breaths. If you should ever feel dizzy, stop the exercise. When you return to this exercise, increase the count of the exhale. (In for 8, Out for 6)

Reverse Breathing to a Syncopated Count - Focus

What to do:

As you breathe in, count to 4. When you breathe out count to 8. If you ever feel that you are not getting enough air, stop the exercise. When you return to this exercise, increase the count of the inhale. (In for 6, Out for 8)

Name that Distraction – Focus

How to do:

Take a deep breath and relax the body. Focus on the breath. When you lose contact with the breath, name that distraction. Did a car honk? Silently say to yourself, "Car honking." Then go back to focusing on your breath. Did a worry come up? Say to yourself, "_____ worry." Thank your mind for reminding you about this, but tell it that now is not the right time. Return to focusing on the breath. Don't judge what comes up. Just acknowledge its presence and continue with your breathing.

Observation Meditations

Concentration

Chapter 2

Observation Meditations

White/Silver Light – Calming

How to do:

Imagine a white light shining above your head. As you breathe in, allow this light to enter the top of your head and slowly flow down the body. As you breathe out, push the darkness out through your bottom. Slowly wash the inside of your body with this light.

In the shower – Calming

How to do:

While in the shower, imagine the water is cleansing you of all negativity. Feel the water as it runs down your head and back, and legs. Visualize this negativity washing down the drain.

Bye-Bye Worries – Calming

How to do:

Take a deep breath. Bring your worry to the front of your mind. Now imagine a cloud, a leaf blowing in the wind, or a stick flowing down a stream. Place your worry on this cloud, leaf or stick and watch it float away from you.

Eating Meditation – Calming

How to do:

Take a deep breath. Examine the next bite you will be taking. What textures does it have? What colors? Smell this bite. Deeply breathe in the aroma. Place the bite into your mouth. How does it feel? Begin chewing very slowly. Notice the flavors. Continue to chew for as long as possible without swallowing. Decide to swallow this bite.

Scanning the Body - Relaxing

How to do:

Breathe in through the nose and out through the mouth 2 times.

- Breathe into the forehead. As you breathe out relax.
- Breathe into the face. Breathe out, relax.
- Breathe into the neck and shoulders. Breathe out, relax.
- Breathe into the heart. Breathe out, relax
- Breathe into the belly. Breathe out, relax.
- Breath into the legs. Breathe out, relax.
- Breathe into the ankles and feet. Breathe out, relax.

Go to sleep – Relaxing

How to do:

Take 3 breaths in through the nose and exhale out through the mouth. Slowly scan the body starting with the feet.

- Breathe in through the nose and notice the feet. Breathe out through the mouth and relax the feet. Silently tell them, "Go to Sleep."
- Breathe in through the nose and notice the legs. Breathe out through the mouth and relax the legs. Silently tell them, "Go to Sleep."
- Breath in through the nose and notice the pelvis area. Breath out through the mouth and relax the buttock and pelvis. Silently tell them, "Go to Sleep."
- Breath in through the nose and notice the back. Breathe out through the mouth and relax the back. Silently tell it "Go to Sleep."
- Breath in through the nose and notice the shoulders. Breathe out through the mouth and relax the shoulders. Silently tell them, "Go to Sleep."

- Breathe in through the nose and notice the neck. Breathe out through the mouth and relax the neck. Silently tell it, "Go to Sleep."

- Breathe in through the nose and notice the face. Breathe out through the mouth and relax the face. Silently tell it, "Go to Sleep."

- Breathe in through the nose and notice the brain. Breathe out through the mouth and relax the brain. Silently tell it, "Go to Sleep."

If you are still awake, repeat until you do fall asleep.

What am I Thinking? - Focus

How to do:

Focus on your thoughts. Notice what the inner voice is saying. Is it negative? Is it judging? Is it rerunning an event from the past? Is it wishing for the future? Just notice. Don't strive to stop it.

What Emotions am I Feeling? - Focus

How to do:

Focus on your emotions. Notice what is churning in your inner world. Am I bored? Am I anxious? Am I excited? Am I calm? Don't judge it – Name it. Notice what happens when that emotion is acknowledged and named.

What Sensations am I Feeling? - Focus

How to do:

Focus on your skin. Can you feel where your clothes touch your skin? Can you feel your socks incasing your feet? Do you have an itch? Is there a pain anywhere? Can you feel the alignment of your posture? Note the sensations without judgment and keep scanning your body.

Walking
Meditations

Concentration

Chapter 3

Walking Meditations

Standing Pose – Compassion

What to do:

Become aware of your feet. Imaging that roots are growing down into the center of the earth. As you breathe in imagine the heat at the earth's core is rising up through the roots and up into your feet and into your legs. Continue to breathe. With each breath, feel the heat rise all the way to your heart. Enjoy this luscious feeling and carry it through your day.

Standing Pose – Relaxing

What to do:

While standing, become aware of your feet. Notice the tension throughout your body. Do a mental checklist from top to bottom or bottom to top relaxing each body part as you scan the body. Example: Feel the top of the head - relax the top of the head. Feel the forehead – relax the forehead. Feel the jaw – relax the jaw. Feel the neck – relax the neck. Feel the shoulders – relax the shoulders. If time does not allow you to scan the whole body, start from the other direction next time.

Swinging – Relaxing

How to do:

Stand with feet shoulder width apart. Twist at the waist and swing the arms so that one is in front of you and one is behind you. As you swing, relax the arms and shoulders. When fully relaxed, the arms will flop into the body as you twist. If you feel dizzy, just keep your head still and focus your eyes on one object as you twist.

One Sense at a Time – Focus

How to do:

Pick a sense – like hearing or smelling – notice all the sounds or smells in the environment as you walk.Pick a color – notice how many things in the environment are that color.

Backwards Walking - Focus

How to do:

Without looking behind you, step backwards with the toe touching the ground and the heel held high. Slowly lower the heel feeling for any thing that will unbalance you. If you feel an obstacle, lift the foot and step backwards again.

Rolling a ball - Focus

How to do:

Imagine that you are walking inside a ball. In order to go straight, you must place one foot directly in front of the other. Each foot will roll from heel to toe as it moves forward.

Distant Point – Focus

How to do:

Pick out an object in the distance. Focus your eyes on this object. If you glance sideways or become distracted by thoughts, return your focus to the item you selected. When you get to the selected point, choose another distant point to focus on for the next segment of your journey.

Next step – Focus

How to do:

As you walk, focus on the ground just a few feet in front of you. Watch as you make your next step. If you look up or get distracted, focus your eyes back to the ground where you will be taking your next step.

Grounding - Focus

How to do:

Become aware of your feet. Every time you place a foot on the ground *feel* your foot touching the ground. Notice the heel touching first and the foot rocking toward the toes. Relax into each step. When you lift your foot up off the ground *feel* the weightlessness of the foot flying through mid-air. Notice the sock as it hugs your foot through the process of one step. Can you feel the inside of your shoe? Continue until you reach your destination.

Added twist! Feel all the way up your leg. Feel the ankle, the shin muscles, the knee, the thigh, and the hip socket working and resting as you walk.

Counting Steps - Focus

How to do:

Become aware of your feet. Place your right foot down and count 1. Then place your left foot down and count 2. Continue counting until you reach your destination. If you become distracted or space out and lose count, begin again – with no judgments.

Silent Mantra Meditations

Concentration

Chapter 4

Silent Mantra Meditations

Gratitude Mantra – Peace of Mind

How to do:

Mentally note every time an unexpected good thing happens with a "Thank You." "Thank you for the parking space." "Thank you for the elevator opening just in time." "Thank you for the taxi that just happened to be driving by."

"I AM" Mantra – Peace of Mind

How to do:

Start with eyes closed. Choose a positive statement that you want to impress upon your subconscious. If you feel scattered, choose a mantra like, "I AM Balanced." If you wish to work on issues of worth, choose a mantra like, "I AM worthy of love, joy and prosperity." Here is a selection of other "I AM" mantras to choose from. Feel free to create a mantra for yourself.

I AM Loved

I AM Beautiful

I AM Strong

I AM Flexible

I AM Lovable

I AM Joyous

I AM Peaceful

I AM Valuable

I AM a unique and beautiful expression of the Divine.

I AM Creative

I AM Safe and Protected in all ways.

I AM Healthy

I AM Complete

Awareness
Meditations

Breath
Meditations

Awareness

Chapter 5

Breath Meditations

Leaving Work at Work – Calming

How to do:

Take a deep breath. Now choose 3 things that you will put away everyday. Pencil in the drawer, stapler on the side of the desk, and tomorrow's paperwork neatly placed in the inbox – or wrench, hammer, and sockets put in their place. Grab your bag and deeply exhale all the day's energy. Imagine everything associated with work is pouring out and off of you into a puddle on the floor. As you walk through the door, another exaggerated exhale and leave the building with mind cleansed.

Fire Breath – Energizing

How to do:

Inhale slowly and deeply through the nose. Then snap your diaphragm up – shooting out a short breath through the nose. Do the repetitions quickly. Continue for 10-15 breaths.

Super Energizer - Energizing

How to do:

Breathe in through the mouth for the count of 4. Breath out through the nose for the count of 4. Continue for 7-8 breaths.

Opening the Mind – Creativity

How to do:

Notice your personal space or "bubble." As you breathe, try to expand that bubble as far as is comfortable. Can you expand your bubble to fill the space you are in? How far can you expand your personal space? Can you fill the isle of the store you are in? Can you fill the whole store from floor to ceiling? If a thought comes up, name it and go back to noticing your personal space.

Just
Breathe

6

Observation Meditations

Awareness

Chapter 6

Observation Meditations

Picture Therapy – Calm

How to do:

Keep a picture in your purse or wallet of a place that brings you joy. It could be a beach scene from a vacation you took, a forest path you walk daily, or a park down the street. Every time you feel a negative emotion, pull out the picture and reconnect with the positive and happy feelings from this place.

Golden Light – Energizing

How to do:

Imagine a golden light focused on your belly button. Breathe this light into your body. Let it fill your legs, torso, and up into your head.

Experiencing a Shower – Creativity

How to do:

As you step into the shower open your awareness to all that is happening. Do you hear the water? Do you smell the soap? Do you feel the water as it hits your body and runs down your back? Do you see the color of the towel. How many things can you experience at the same time?

Sensing Inner and Outer - Intuition

How to do:

Try to find a point of balance between the inner and outer experience. Can you be aware of your emotions and the bird singing? Can you find a balance between the foot connecting with the ground, the emotions, the person coming your way, and the bird singing? Begin with one inner item and one outer item. Add an inner and outer item as you master each additional set.

Heart meditation - Compassion

How to do:

Gently rub your hands together. Place your right hand over your heart and place your left hand on top of your right hand. Imagine your heart glowing with radiant energy. Imagine your body filling with this energy. Open yourself so that this loving energy can radiate out into the world.

Naming the Judgment - Judging

How to do:

The object is to quickly judge each item as <u>Pleasant</u>, <u>Unpleasant</u> or <u>Neutral</u> and move to the next item. Don't get caught up in the narrative of, "I want that," or "How rude of someone to dump trash here!." Don't let your mind-puppy chase that rabbit. Notice what you notice in your environment. Once something comes up, silently in your mind quickly judge that item as <u>Pleasant</u>, <u>Unpleasant</u>, or <u>Neutral</u> then move on to the next item.

Gratitude – Judging

How to do:

Make a list of things you are grateful for or all the good things that have happened today. Proof of goodness in our life can change our mindset.

A man of calm

is like a shady tree.

People who need shelter

come to it.

-Toba Beta

Awareness

Walking
Meditations

Awareness

Chapter 7

Walking Meditations

Caution! These meditations need to be done in environments that are safe and free of cars or other hazards. These meditations are not meant for busy parking lots or rugged hiking trails.

Environmental Awareness – Relaxing

How to do:

Open the awareness to the soothing effects of the sun and the air on your skin. Can you feel that you are a part of the wholeness of life?

Extra Credit:

Add experiencing the breath to your awareness.

Softening the Eyes - Relaxing

How to do:

As you walk, open the peripheral vision. Watch the panoramic view as it slowly fades behind you. This will relax the eyes, which relaxes the body.

Sounds – Creativity

How to do:

As you walk, listen to the sounds in your environment. Hear each sound fully. How many different sounds can you pick out?

Full Awareness - Creativity

How to do:

How many things can you be aware of without judging or bringing your attention to one item? Can you be aware of a bird, a car driving by, a person walking toward you, and your bodily sensations of walking, all at the same time? If you get distracted, note why this happened – without judgment of yourself or the distracting event - and begin again.

Colors – Creativity

How to do:

As you walk, notice all the colors in your environment. Note the differences in hue and concentration. How many different colors can you pick out?

Fill the Space - Intuition

How to do:

Notice your personal space or "bubble." As you walk, try to expand that bubble as far as is comfortable. Can you expand your bubble to fill the space you are in? How far can you expand your personal space? Can you fill the isle of the store you are in? Can you fill the whole store from floor to ceiling?

Added Twist:

Can you expand to cover the block you live on? Can you expand enough to fill your city, state, country, and finally the whole planet or whole universe?

Don't Seek,

Don't search,

Don't ask,

Don't demand - relax.

Don't knock.

If you relax, it comes.

If you relax, it is there.

If you relax,

you start vibrating with it.

-Osho

Awareness

Silent Mantra Meditations

Awareness

Chapter 8

Silent Mantra Meditations

I rest in stillness – Calming

How to do:

Close your eyes and expand your personal bubble to a comfortably large size. Silently repeat, "I rest in stillness."

It's ALL GOOD Mantra – Peace of Mind

How to do:

When something happens that brings an automatic negative mental response, use this question, "What is *Good* about this?" Make the brain think of reasons why it is good to be stuck in traffic. Why is it good that I must pay taxes?

The Irritating Person Mantra – Release Judgment

How to do:

Take a deep breath. Repeat, "___Say the person's name____ is valuable and needed just the way they are." If your mind questions this statement, remind it of all the good qualities of this person.

Peace, Love, or Compassion Mantra – Compassion

How to do:

Start with eyes closed. Bring into your awareness a feeling such as Peace, Love, or Compassion. Repeat the word that reflects the feeling you have chosen. Expand that awareness as far as possible while still repeating the word you have chosen. Fill the room you are in. Fill the whole building with Peace, Love, or Compassion.

Every experience,

no matter how bad it seems,

Holds within it a blessing of some kind.

The goal is to find it.

-Buddha

Awareness

Conclusion

Chapter 9

Conclusion

When you first look at these meditations, it can seem that they are not real meditations. They require no effort. However, the proof of the method can be found in the question, "Did they work?" Were you able to get your puppy-mind out of the same old rut? Watch for progress. This is a long term practice with long term benefits. After a couple of days, do you feel calmer and clearer? If so, then these meditations have performed the function they were designed to accomplish.

There is no such thing as perfect happiness, but there is "happier than before." Keeping track of your meditations and your experiences will help you chart your puppy-mind's successes. I have created a whole line of meditation journals specifically for this purpose. You can visit the Aashni Spiritual Living website or find the complete collection of meditation journals on Amazon.com.

About the Author

Mischa V Alyea was introduced to meditation in 1998. As a busy mother of three, she did not have time to spend hours each day meditating. She soon realized that tiny meditations throughout the day worked as well, if not better, than hour-long meditation sessions. Now that the children are grown and settled in their own lives, Mischa is filling you in on the secret of mini-meditations that she has used for many years.

She lives in Kansas City with her husband and Sushi the infamous house monster.

We invite you to select your next journal
from our growing line of products
for meditation enthusiasts.

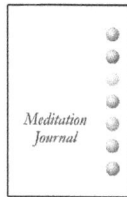

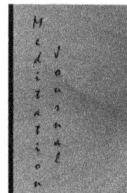

Visit our website for a complete listing

www.AashniSpiritualLiving.com/Journals

Aashni
Spiritual Living

Visit us at:

www.AashniSpiritualLiving.com

www.ingramcontent.com/pod-product-compliance
Lightning Source LLC
Chambersburg PA
CBHW071433040426
42445CB00012BA/1353